C000089157

THE LITTLE BOOK OF
CELTIC LORE

In the same series

THE LITTLE BOOK OF
CELTIC
LORE

Compiled by
CAITLÍN AND JOHN MATTHEWS

ELEMENT

Shaftesbury, Dorset ✦ Boston, Massachusetts
Melbourne, Victoria

Compiled by Caitlín and John Matthews

© ELEMENT BOOKS LIMITED 1998
© ORIGINAL TEXT CAITLIN AND JOHN MATTHEWS 1998

Published in Great Britain in 1998 by
ELEMENT BOOKS LIMITED
Shaftesbury, Dorset SP7 8BP

Published in the USA in 1998 by
ELEMENT BOOKS INC.
160 North Washington Street, Boston, MA 02114

Published in Australia in 1998 by
ELEMENT BOOKS
and distributed by
PENGUIN AUSTRALIA LTD
487 Maroondah Highway, Ringwood, Victoria 3134

Designed and Created for ELEMENT BOOKS
By THE BRIDGEWATER BOOK COMPANY LTD

Printed and bound in Singapore
British Library Cataloguing in Publication data available
Library of Congress Cataloging in Publication data available

ISBN 1 86204 229 2

The publishers would like to thank the following for the use of pictures:
Cameron Collection: Title Page, 29
The Stockmarket: 21, 47
Stuart Littlejohn, Crediton: 36

CONTENTS

A CELTIC TAPESTRY

In this little book, we have woven together some of the threads which pattern the Celtic loom of existence. Our tapestry explores five dimensions, drawing upon some of the names which the ancient Celts gave to the worlds beyond earthly existence. The Land of the Living explores the nature of our communion with the land and with life. The Land of Youth explores the heroic adventures of life's quest. On the Plain of Delight we linger to overhear the whispering of lovers. On the Plain of Silver we reawaken the memory of our deep vision. In the Land of Promise we may still glimpse the patterns of eternal wisdom.

For the Celts, there was no separation between the worlds of humanity and that of the spirits and creatures, or between nature and the subtle weaving of creation. Love and war, vision and struggle were lived out within the encompassing of the elements.

Their writings drew upon an oral, living tradition whose vision still casts its spell today.

The material selected here is drawn from ancient and modern Celtic sources, with many fresh translations by ourselves.

CATLÍN AND JOHN MATTHEWS

The LAND OF THE LIVING
∞ TIR NA MBEO ∞

Our journey begins in the Land of the Living, at sunrise. It proceeds ever in a sunwise direction, following the sacred circuit of the year through time and space. It is marked by the invocation of the powers of the universe, to clothe the traveler with a garment of spiritual protection:

> I arise today
> Through the strength of heaven:
> Light of sun,
> Radiance of moon,
> Splendor of fire,
> Speed of lightning,
> Swiftness of wind,
> Depth of sea,
> Stability of earth,
> Firmness of rock. [1]

Interwoven with the ninefold elements of the universe, the supplicant becomes identified with these powers, even taking them to be his judge:

> I will keep faith until the sky falls upon me and crushes me, until the earth opens and swallows me, until the seas arise and overwhelm me. [2]

So runs the awesome oath, appealing to the elements as the foundations of the universe, to be the enduring witnesses to human promises. The elements are witnesses of all ritual action: the many-colored winds bringing different gifts and opportunities; fire and water are used by midwives to sain new-born children and by healers to cleanse people and animals of sickness; the sun and moon cast pathways of light upon the circuits of life; hills, rocks and waters are everywhere reverenced as nodes of power and memory, givers of initiation, treasure and song. For this is the Land of the Living.

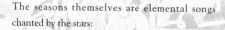

The seasons themselves are elemental songs
chanted by the stars:

> Wind comes from the spring star in the East,
> Fire comes from the summer star in the South,
> Water comes from the autumn star in the West,
> Wisdom, silence and death come from the winter
> star in the North. [3]

In the prayer of the Four Stars of Destiny, the stars
are the fourfold cloaks worn upon the circuit of life,

> Reul Near, Star of the East,
> give us kindly birth;
> Reul Deas, Star of the South,
> give us great love;
> Reul Niari, Star of the West,
> give us quiet age;
> Reul Tuath, Star of the North,
> give us death. [4]

The changing seasons teach us of both life and death, forming the web of our understanding, becoming the regulators of our mood. In his wanderings in the Caledonian Forest, Merlin, afflicted by madness after a cruel battle, rebels against the winter which too closely reflects his own bare soul:

> O that here were no winter or white frost!
> That it were spring or summer, and that
> the cuckoo would come back singing, and the
> nightingale who softens sad hearts with her
> devoted song... and that in new foliage other
> birds should sing in harmonious measures,
> delighting me with their music, while a
> new earth should breathe forth odors from
> new flowers under the green grass. [5]

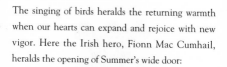

The singing of birds heralds the returning warmth when our hearts can expand and rejoice with new vigor. Here the Irish hero, Fionn Mac Cumhail, heralds the opening of Summer's wide door:

> May: fair-aspected,
>   perfect season:
>   blackbirds sing
>   where the sun glows.

> The hardy cuckoo calls
>   a welcome to noble Summer:
>   ends the bitter storms
>   that strip the trees of the wood.

> Summer cuts the streams:
>   swift horses seek water:
>   the heather grows tall:
>   fair foliage flourishes.

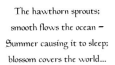

The hawthorn sprouts:
smooth flows the ocean –
Summer causing it to sleep:
blossom covers the world...

The true man sings
gladly in the bright day,
sings loudly of May –
fair–aspected season. [6]

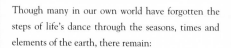

Though many in our own world have forgotten the steps of life's dance through the seasons, times and elements of the earth, there remain:

> that small untoward clan, which knows the
> divine call of the spirit through the brain, and
> the secret whisper of the soul in the heart, and
> for ever perceives the veil of mystery and the
> rainbows of hope upon our human horizons,
> which hears and sees, and yet turns wisely,
> meanwhile, to the life of the green earth, of
> which we are part, to the common kindred of
> living things with which we are at one. [7]

The Land of the Living teaches its lesson in simple ways, reminding us that the conscious and remembering spirit of the universe survives in all created life forms. But the apparent fragility of the living web cloaks an immense strength which can still be gratefully acknowledged:

Three slender things that best support the
world: the slender stream of milk from the
cow's dug into the pail; the slender blade of
green corn upon the ground; the slender thread
over the hand of a skilled woman. [8]

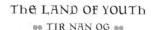

THE LAND OF YOUTH
∞ TIR NAN OG ∞

To be young in those times was to be a hero; to be a hero was to prove oneself the best: born in strange circumstances, living by wondrous laws, achieving marvelous feats, the Celtic heroes and warriors revealed their prowess early. Here, the youthful Culhwch rides to his uncle Arthur's court:

> The youth pricked forth upon a steed with head dappled gray, of four winters old, firm of limb, with shell-formed hoofs, having a bridle of linked gold on his head, and upon him a saddle of costly gold. And in the youth's hand were two spears of silver, sharp, well-tempered, headed with steel, three ells in length, of an edge to wound the wind, and cause blood to flow, and swifter than the fall of a dewdrop from the blade of reedgrass upon

the earth when the dew of June is at the
heaviest. A gold-hilted sword was upon his
thigh, the blade of which was of gold... of the
hue of the lightning of heaven: his war horn

was of ivory. Before him were two brindled
white-breasted grayhounds, having strong
collars of rubies about their necks, reaching
from the shoulder to the ear. And the one that
was on the left side bounded across to the

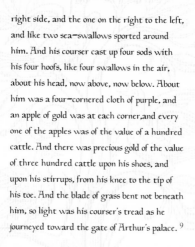

right side, and the one on the right to the left,
and like two sea-swallows sported around
him. And his courser cast up four sods with
his four hoofs, like four swallows in the air,
about his head, now above, now below. About
him was a four-cornered cloth of purple, and
an apple of gold was at each corner, and every
one of the apples was of the value of a hundred
cattle. And there was precious gold of the value
of three hundred cattle upon his shoes, and
upon his stirrups, from his knee to the tip of
his toe. And the blade of grass bent not beneath
him, so light was his courser's tread as he
journeyed toward the gate of Arthur's palace. [9]

All heroes were proclaimed at birth to be aston-
ishing. Cuchulainn slew the great hound of Culainn
the Smith and received his name, which means
'Hound of Culainn', as a result. While still a child
he mastered the finest chariot horses in the King of

Ireland's stable; his skills and his strength were both prodigious. Fionn, Ireland's other great champion, was always of a more meditative mien, though his abilities were nonetheless considerable. Placed in the charge of two women warriors (and the warrior women of the Celts were even more ferocious and terrifying than their men!), he soon displayed his remarkable skills and founded a band of premier warriors known as the Fianna, whose motto was, 'Truth in our hearts. Strength in our hands. Consistency in our tongues.' The training of the Fianna reflected their leader's own abilities:

> There was no man taken until he knew
> twelve books of poetry. And before any man
> was accepted, he would be put into a deep hole
> in the ground up to his middle, and he having
> his shield and hazel rod in his hand. And nine
> men would go the length of ten furrows from
> him and would cast their spears at him at the

same time. And if he got a wound from one of
them he was not thought fit to join with the
Fianna. And after that his hair would be
fastened up, and he put to run through the
woods of Ireland, and the Fianna following
after him to try could they wound him, and
only the length of the branch between
themselves and himself when they started.
And if they came up with him and wounded
him, he was not let join them; or if his spears
trembled in his hand, or if a branch of a tree
had undone the plaiting of his hair, or if he
had cracked a dry stick under his foot, and he
running. And they would not take him among
them till he had made a leap over a stick the
height of himself, and till he had stooped under
one the height of his knee, and till he had
taken a thorn out of his foot with his nail, and
he running his fastest. But if he had done all
these things, he was of Fionn's people. [10]

Such things were the norm among the bright ranks of the heroes. But they knew other ways as well, and were gentle by turns, and wise. Cormac, known as the Irish Solomon, gave a list of things that pertained both to king and warrior:

> Be not too wise, nor too foolish,
> be not too conceited, nor too diffident,
> be not too haughty, nor too humble,
> be not too talkative, nor too silent,
> be not too hard, nor too feeble.

for:

> If you be too wise, one will expect too much of you;
> if you be foolish, you will be deceived;
> if you be too conceited, you will be thought vexatious;
> if you be too humble, you will be without honor;
> if you be too talkative, you will not be heeded;
> if you be too silent, you will not be regarded;
> if you be too hard, you will be broken;
> if you be too feeble, you will be crushed.

'It is through these habits,' adds Cormac, 'that the young become old and kingly warriors' [11]

But many did not reach old age. When the hero passed early to the Land of Promise, he was remembered by the women for his beauty and by the men for his battle skills, as in this lament for the great hero-king Niall of the Nine Hostages:

Eyelashes black, delicate, equal in beauty,
and dark eyebrows:
The crown of the woad, a bright hyacinth:
That was the color of his pupils.
The colour of his cheeks at all seasons, even
and symmetrical:
The fox-glove, the blood of a calf – a feast
without flaw!
The crown of the forest in May.

His white teeth, his red lips that never
reproved in anger
His shape like a fiery blaze
Overtopping the warriors of Erin.

Like the moon, like the sun, like a fiery beacon
Was the splendor of Niall:
Like a dragon-ship from the wave without a flaw
Was Niall, Echu's son.

Darling hero of the shining host!
Whose tribes are vast, a beloved band:
Every man was under protection when
We used to go to foregather with him. [12]

The PLAIN OF DELIGHT
∞ MAG MELL ∞

There are three sparks that kindle love: a face, demeanor, speech. Any of these can bring us to Mag Mell, the Plain of Delight, the home of many lovers: Trystan and Esyllt, Diarmuid and Grainne, Culhwch and Olwen, names that still evoke a shiver of delight, as we witness their still living beauty and their often woeful fate. Who could fail to love Olwen, 'White Footprint', as she appears in the old Welsh tale of Culhwch.

> The maiden was clothed in a robe of flame—
> colored silk, and about her neck was a collar of
> ruddy gold on which were precious emeralds
> and rubies. More yellow was her head than
> the flower of the broom, and her skin was
> whiter than the foam of the wave, and fairer
> were her hands and her fingers than the

blossom of the wood anemone amidst the spray
of the meadow fountain. The eye of the trained
hawk, the glance of the thrice-mewed falcon
was not brighter than hers. her breast was
more snowy than the breast of the white
swan, her cheek was redder than the reddest
roses. Whoso beheld her was filled with her
love. Four white trefoils sprang up wherever
she trod. [13]

Culhwch fell in love with Olwen before ever he saw
and won her, but her heart was willing. Yet it was
otherwise when the Welsh enchanters, Math and
Gwydion, made a wife out of flowers for their
kinsman, Llew Llaw Gyffes, whose mother had
sworn he should never marry a mortal woman. In
conjuring Blodeuwedd from 'the blossom of the oak,
and the blossoms of the broom, and the blossoms of
the meadow sweet,' they produced 'a maiden, the
fairest and most graceful that ever man saw,' but

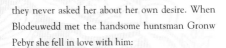

they never asked her about her own desire. When
Blodeuwedd met the handsome huntsman Gronw
Pebyr she fell in love with him:

> And he gazed on her, and the same
> thought came unto him as unto her,
> so that he could not conceal from her
> that he loved her, but he declared
> unto her that he did so. Thereupon she
> was very joyful. And all their discourse
> that night was concerning the
> affection and love which they felt one
> for the other, and which in no longer
> space than one evening had arisen. [14]

Like many another, their love was doomed; for
when their plot to kill Llew was discovered, Gronw
paid the price with his death, and Blodeuwedd was
turned into an owl by her vengeful conjurors.

Love could be perilous, overlooking the bonds of marriage, especially if the otherworldly powers were involved. Diarmuid O'Duibhne, one of Fionn's Fianna, was already handsome, but he was further gifted with a love-spot upon his forehead by a faery woman; such was its power to seduce, that no woman could resist it, and Diarmuid had to wear a hat over his brows lest he cause marital confusion wherever he went. But when he met the bride of his lord, Fionn McCumhail:

> It chanced...the cap fell from him, and Grainne was looking out at him as it fell, and great love for him came on her there and then. And she called her serving-maid to her, and bade her bring the great golden cup that held drink for nine times nine men from the sunny house. And when the serving-maid brought the cup, she filled it with wine that had enchantment in it... And all that drank of it fell into the same

heavy sleep. And when they were all in their
sleep, Grainne rose up softly from the seat
where she was, and she turned her face to
Diarmuid and she said: 'Will you take my love,
Diarmuid son of Duibhne, and will you bring me
away out of this house tonight?' 15

They fled to the wild places together until a reconciliation was arranged with Fionn, at whose jealous hands Diarmuid came to his death. Jealousy, too, drove King March, whose wife, Esyllt, fell in love with the handsome stranger, Trystan, to pursue them when they fled into the Forest of Celyddon. When they would not come out, March complained to Arthur, who sent men to demand of Trystan that he give up Esyllt. Trystan would not, yet peace was made in the end through a strange bargain:

> Arthur conversed with the two of them in turn, and neither of them was willing to be without Esyllt. Then Arthur adjudged her to one while the leaves should be on the wood, and to the other during the time that the leaves should not be on the wood, the husband to have the choice. And the latter chose the time when the leaves should not be on the wood, because the night is longest during that season. And Arthur announced that to Esyllt, and she said: 'Blessed be the judgement and he who gave it!'

And Esyllt sang this englynní (verse):

> Three trees are good in nature:
> the holly, the ivy and the yew,
> they keep their leaves throughout their lives:
> I am Trystan's as long as he lives. [16]

Love, doomed or fulfilled, is a bright thread in the weaving. Aengus Og, god of love and youthfulness, kindles death and life in the hearts of his subjects:

> There is an old legend that Aengus goes to and fro upon the world, a weaver of rainbows...he is a deathless comrade of the Spring, and we may well pray to him to let his green fire move in our veins: whether he be but the Eternal Youth of the world, or be also Love, whose soul is youth: or even though he be likewise Death himself, Death to whom Love was wedded long, long ago. [17]

The PLAIN OF SILVER
∞ MAG ARGATNAL ∞

We come to the Plain of Silver, which is also the place of vision, magic and enchantment. It is the place we enter naturally at twilight, when the worlds mesh and meld at the between lights: without its necessary enchantment we lose touch with the on-going story of our soul which is enriched and enlightened by whatever we experience upon our journey. We do not fear to enter night, for there are ever

Three candles that illume every darkness:
truth, nature, knowledge. [18]

All creativity begins upon the Plain of Silver, as the onset of darkness heralds the telling of tales. We hearken to stories of kings, queens, younger sons and daughters, magical beasts, quests and dangers, monsters and faeries, and forget our own troubles,

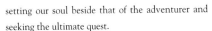

setting our soul beside that of the adventurer and seeking the ultimate quest.

Those who have no stories, sing no songs, are poor indeed. But however scanty our store of treasure, we can always access the door of dreams for soul's enrichment:

had I the heaven's embroidered cloths,
Emwrought with golden and silver light,
The blue and the dim and the dark cloths
Of night and light and the half-light,
I would spread the cloths under your feet:
But I, being poor, have only my dreams:
I have spread my dreams under your feet:
Tread softly because you tread on my dreams. [19]

The Celtic poet is in tune with the universe, able to access any level of its connected life-forms and to draw back wandering souls into the nets of the story once again. The poet is a prophet, a kist of knowledge, the memory of the people, a shaman who draws upon the spirits of the universe.

As Amergin Whiteknee, chief poet and shaman of the Milesian invaders, greets the land of Ireland from his ship, he remembers all existences of which he has partaken in flesh and in vision. He makes this rhapsodic song of self-introduction to the land, speaking of his creative powers by way of strange kennings: of the cattle of Tethra as the stars arising from the sea, greeting the ox of the moon:

> I am a wind on the sea,
> I am a wave of the ocean,
> I am the roar of the sea,
> I am an ox of seven exiles,
> I am a hawk on a cliff,

I am a tear of the sun,

I am a turning in a maze,

I am a boar in valor,

I am a salmon in a pool,

I am a lake on a plain,

I am a dispensing power,

I am a spirit of skilful gift,

I am a grass-blade giving decay to the earth,

I am a creative god giving inspiration.

Who else clears the stones of the mountain?

Who is it who declaims the sun's arising?

Who is it who tells where the sun sets?

Who brings cattle from the house of Tethra?

Upon whom do the cattle of Tethra smile?

Who is this ox?

Who is the weaving god who mends the
thatch of wounds?

– The incantation of a spear,

– The incantation of the wind. [20]

In Amergin's mystical identification with all things, he becomes one of the physicians of the soul, reweaving the scattered elements of life into a new wholeness. This is the task of Celtic poets, whose skill is to bring the soul to the point of vision, rest, and stillness. The music of their healing skill is known by three strains: the laugh strain, which raises the spirits; the sorrow strain, which causes the release of tears; and the sleep strain, which brings rest to troubled souls.

Sometimes the soul goes for healing into the body of a creature. There are many who endured from earliest times by this means, to have the companionship of other creatures than humans. This primal knowledge endowed the transmigrant with great power of memory. Tuan mac Carill is one such who has traveled a circuit of births in different shapes. The last survivor of his race, he continues as a stag, boar, hawk and salmon and is able to relate the history of Ireland to those who come afterward. He experiences the vigor of each animal:

> I was king of the boar-herds in Ireland, and I still went the round of my abode when I used to come into this land of Ulster at the time of my old age and wretchedness; for in the same place I changed into all these shapes. Therefore I always visited that place to await the renewal.... I remembered every shape in which I had been before. [21]

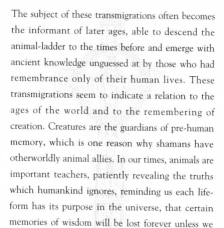

The subject of these transmigrations often becomes the informant of later ages, able to descend the animal-ladder to the times before and emerge with ancient knowledge unguessed at by those who had remembrance only of their human lives. These transmigrations seem to indicate a relation to the ages of the world and to the remembering of creation. Creatures are the guardians of pre-human memory, which is one reason why shamans have otherworldly animal allies. In our times, animals are important teachers, patiently revealing the truths which humankind ignores, reminding us each life-form has its purpose in the universe, that certain memories of wisdom will be lost forever unless we reconnect with the enchantment which feeds the soul.

The Plain of Silver restores us to memory, as Merlin is restored to himself by the poet Taliesin, who therapeutically recreates the universe for his friend in bardic incantation. Merlin's soul returns to him and he cries:

Oh King, through whom the order of the
starry heavens exists, through whom the sea
and the land with its pleasing grass give forth
and nourish their offspring and with their
profuse fertility give frequent aid to mankind...
I was carried away from myself and like a
spirit I knew the acts of past peoples and
predicted the future. Then since I knew the
secrets of things and the flight of birds and
the wandering motions of the stars and the
gliding of the fishes, all this vexed me and
denied a natural rest to my human mind by a
severe law. Now I have come to myself... [22]

Many of us hopelessly contemplate,

The world without wonder, the world
without mystery! That indeed is the rainbow
without colors, the sunrise without living gold,
the noon void of light... [23]

How can the soul or the world be re-enchanted once it has lost its grasp of the golden links of tradition? Can we catch the old song which restores the enchantment? Celtic story speaks of seven questers who return from the perilous inner journey to bring cauldron or Grail back from the innerworlds.

> And such joy did (they) bring about, that thereupon did the people repeople the land after the great destruction... and the waters which ran not, and the fountains which flowed not, for that they had been dried up, ran forth amidst the meadows. Then were the fields green and bountiful, and the woods clad in leaves the day that the Court of Joy was found. [24]

The Court of Joy, wherein the restoring vessel abides, can still be discovered. The wisdom of the ancient earth's enchantment still resounds in the deep recesses of the human heart, leading us to memory and gladness.

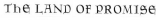

The LAND OF PROMISE
∞ TIR TAIRNGIRE ∞

The Land of Promise is also called the Land of Heart's Desire. The restlessness of divine discontent usually presages the journey to this land wherein we discover that such a desire is only the fulfilment of our deepest nature:

> The desire of the faery women: dew.
>
> The desire of the faery host: wind.
>
> The desire of the raven: blood.
>
> The desire of the snipe: the wilderness.
>
> The desire of the seamew: the lawns of the sea.
>
> The desire of the poet: the soft low music of
> the Tribe of the Green Mantles.
>
> The desire of man: the love of woman.
>
> The desire of women: the little clan.
>
> The desire of the soul: wisdom. [25]

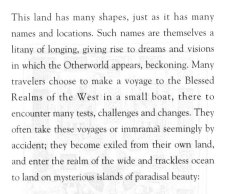

This land has many shapes, just as it has many names and locations. Such names are themselves a litany of longing, giving rise to dreams and visions in which the Otherworld appears, beckoning. Many travelers choose to make a voyage to the Blessed Realms of the West in a small boat, there to encounter many tests, challenges and changes. They often take these voyages or *immramaí* seemingly by accident; they become exiled from their own land, and enter the realm of the wide and trackless ocean to land on mysterious islands of paradisal beauty:

An ancient tree there is in bloom,
On which birds call to the hours:
In harmony of song they all are wont
To chant together every hour.

Colors of every shade glisten
throughout the gentle-voiced plains:
Joy is known, ranked around music,
In silver-cloud plain to the southward.

Unknown is wailing or treachery
In the homely well-tilled land:
There is nothing rough or harsh,
But sweet music striking on the ear.

Without grief, without gloom, without death,
Without any sickness or debility. [26]

This Otherworld of wonders is a still-living dimension to which all mortals can relate. It transcends but also intersects the reality we call 'everyday life.' It is the source from which inspiration comes. It is accessible through that burning glass of the soul – the imagination – which is nothing less than our doorway to the Otherworld, through which come the dreams, visions and ideas which transform ordinary reality. Such thresholds present themselves in our daily life: on the verge of wells, rivers or seas, which the Celtic poets believed to be the place of poetic inspiration.

In the circle of being let this prayer for long life lead us along the streams of inspiration in the fair lands of knowledge, from the Land of Promise back to the Land of the Living:

> I invoke the seven daughters of Ocean
> who weave the threads of the sons of age.
> Three deaths be taken from me,
> three life-times be given me,
> seven waves of surety be granted me.
> No illusions disturb my journey,
> in brilliant breastplate without hurt.
> My honor shall not be bound by oblivion.
> Welcome age! Death shall not corrupt the old.
>
> I invoke the Silver One, undying and deathless,
> may my life be enduring as white-bronze!
> May my double be killed!
> May my rights be upheld!
> May my strength be increased!
> May my grave not be dug!

May death not visit me!

May my journey be fulfilled!

I shall not be devoured by the headless adder,

nor by the hard green tick, nor by the headless
    beetle.

I shall not be injured by a bevy of women nor a
    gang of armed men.

May the King of the Universe stretch time for me!

I invoke Senach of the seven aeons,

fostered by faery women on nurturing breasts.

May my seven candles never be extinguished!

I am an indestructible fortress,

I am an unassailable rock,

I am a precious jewel,

I am the prosperity of the weak.

May I live a hundred times a hundred years,
    each century in turn.

The fullness of their brew my sufficiency!

The encircling of the Spirit's fortress be
    about me! [27]

Our fivefold journey has led us through the looms of life, with courage, love, vision and inspiration as our guides. With these many-colored skeins may we weave the pattern of our spiritual tapestry to give covering for lives yet unborn.

❧ SOURCES ❧

1   Kuno Meyer, *Selections from Ancient Irish Poetry*, Constable & Co., 1913
2   Caitlín Matthews, *The Celtic Book of the Dead*, Harper Collins, 1992
3   Fiona MacLeod, *Iona*, W. Heinemann, 1927
4   *Ibid.*
5   Geoffrey of Monmouth, *Vita Merlini*, trans. J. J. Parry, University of Illinois, 1925
6   trans. John Matthews in *From the Isle of Dreams*, Floris Books, 1993
7   Fiona MacLeod, *The Birds of Angus Og*, W. Heinemann, 1927
8   Kuno Meyer, *op. cit.*
9   Lady Charlotte Guest, *The Mabinogion* (trans.), J.M. Dent, 1937
10 Lady Augusta Gregory, *Gods and Fighting Men*, John Murray, 1904
11 Kuno Meyer, *op. cit.*
12 Adapted by the authors from K. Meyer in *Selections from Ancient Irish Poetry*
13 Lady Charlotte Guest, *op. cit.*
14 *Ibid.*
15 Lady Augusta Gregory, *op. cit.*
16 T.P. Cross (trans. 1912), reprinted in *A Celtic Reader* by John Matthews, Aquarian Press, 1991
17 Fiona MacLeod, *Birds of Angus Og.*
18 Kuno Meyer, *op. cit.*
19 W.B. Yeats, *The Wind Among the Reeds*, 1899.
20 trans. Caitlín Matthews.
21 Scél Túan maic Carill, trans. Kuno Meyer, VOB.
22 Geoffrey of Monmouth, *Vita Merlini.*
23 Fiona McLeod, *Birds of Angus Og.*
24 Sebastian Evans, *In Quest of the Holy Grail*, J.M. Dent, 1898
25 Fiona McLeod, *From the Hills of Dream*, W. Heinemann, 1929
26 Kuno Meyer, *op. cit.*
27 trans. Caitlín Matthews.